CW00839596

JOSHI GOSHIN HO
SELF-DEFENSE FOR WOMEN OF TRADITIONAL JUDO

Authors

© 2019

BRUCE R. BETHERS

JOSE A. CARACENA FERNÁNDEZ

GABRIEL GARCÍA MUÑOZ

© All rights reserved

PRINTED BY BLURB (EE. UU)
2019

DIRECTED AND SUPERVISED BY:

WITH THE SUPPORT AND COLLABORATION OF:

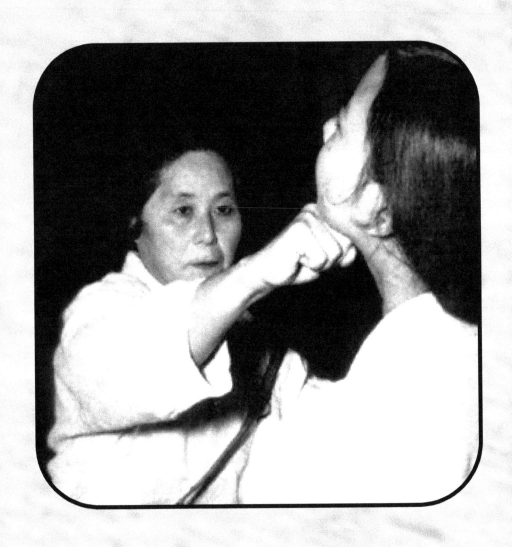

KEIKO FUKUDA SENSEI

"Judo was newly created from Jujitsu, and more importance was put on self-defense rather than on destroying opponents. As Judo developed, more and more emphasis was put on conquering oneself since Judo is based on the philosophy that each technique in its outcome is related to the participant's mind.

In Judo, Randori and Kata are both of equal importance and both are essential to all Judoists. In Kata, one studies the theories and concepts of defense and attack and, therefore, acquires actual knowledge of The methods of self- defense.

However, true Judo does not stop at techniques. The principle of true Judo is in how effectively one defends oneself against an attacking opponent by training one's body and mind rather than by merely defeating the opponent. In other words, Judo is for self-defense and not for attacking, and this objective is especially emphasized in Women's Judo.

Judo techniques are divided into three parts (throwing, holding, and hitting) and there are many variations to each technique. Mental reserve and self-confidence will become greater as one masters these techniques."

KEIKO FUKUDA, 10th DAN

AUTHOR BIOGRAPHIES

Sensei Bruce R. Bethers was born in 1950 in Oklahoma City, OK USA. He first stepped on the mat in 1963 at the Central YMCA in Oklahoma City, studying Kodokan Judo and Japanese Ju-Jitsu. In 1965, he also began training in Shotokan Karate. Among his notable sensei were John Chaffin, Clif Norgaard, Guy Poos & Koichi Kobayashi. He has studied and trained in the martial arts for over 50 years.

His goal was to learn and teach self-defense, however, he later also competed in both Judo and Karate competition. Sensei Bethers grew up working at the YMCA and taught martial arts in nearly every branch of the "Y" in Oklahoma City while in high school and college.

While serving in the U.S. Army in Germany, Sensei Bethers also taught Judo and Ju-Jitsu to soldiers & dependents. During this time, he led the formation of the U.S. Armed Forces Martial Arts Association while in Europe. After his military service, Sensei Bethers worked as a Professional YMCA Director. During his "Y" career, he led the founding of Oklahoma's largest YMCA in Norman, Oklahoma. As the Executive Director for this "Y", he also directed its martial arts program. In 1989, after 11 years working professionally in the YMCA, Sensei Bethers retired from the "Y" and went back on active duty in the U.S. Army. In 2003, he retired with 32 years of military service as an Army Lieutenant Colonel. From 2003 thru 2013, Sensei Bethers worked as a consultant with the U.S. Military in the Pentagon, Washington D.C. and in SW Asia. Since 1999, Sensei Bethers has served as President of United States Ju-Jitsu Federation (USJJF) and since 2005, he has also served as President of USA Traditional Kodokan Judo (USA-TKJ). Sensei Bethers has translated and co-authored several Books on Traditional Kodokan Judo and Japanese Ju-Jitsu.

BRUCE R. BETHERS

JUSHI GOSHIN HO

AUTHOR BIOGRAPHIES

Sensei José Antonio Caracena was born in Madrid, Spain in 1976, starting in Judo in September 1983. He has been training for more than 35 years in Japanese jujutsu, traditional judo and personal defense.

Judo and Jujutsu as sports were never his goal, since he was very young he always cared about all the less known and less practiced aspects of these arts, doing a great job of documentation, research and translation. In the 1990s, he also studied Tenjin Shinyo Ryu Jujutsu, a school considered "the father of Judo".

For years now, his program has been to spread across the world conducting courses, seminars and conferences based on the complete work of Jigoro Kano called "Kano Ryu Nihon Jujutsu". His program consists of studying, practicing and disseminating all the kata, fundamentals and techniques that have fallen into disuse today and that once belonged to Judo, whether created by Jigoro Kano, for his first generation of students in the Kodokan or by outstanding Japanese students of this art. Sensei Caracena has rescued the Torite no kata, Mifune Soen Goshin jutsu, Kime shiki, Joshi Goshinho, Kazuo ito Goshin Jutsu etc.

He is the author of several jujutsu and judo books, some of which have been bestsellers, sold in more than 25 countries and translated into several languages. He is currently an International 6th Dan teacher.

JOSE A. CARACENA

AUTHOR BIOGRAPHIES

Sensei Gabriel García was born in the city of Valencia, Spain, on March 19, 1975. He currently holds the 8th degree of Dan, International Master of Martial Arts.

He started in the practice of Karate and Judo in the 80s, adding to these arts the practice of Japanese Bujutsu. The desire to learn led him to study, over the years to this day, various Martial Arts such as Ninpo, Jujutsu, Kobujutsu, Battojutsu, Kenjutsu, among others and self-defense systems.

In addition, he is passionate about Japanese art and culture and for this reason he started a personal project with the aim of connecting Japan and his Arts with the rest of the world, creating a bridge of communication between them.

He seeks to find the essence of art and this can only be found at its origin: Japan. That is why he has undertaken a path to knowledge (Musha shugyō 武 者 修行), traveling on many occasions to Japan to learn from different traditional schools (Koryū budō 古 流).

That project is called Bugeikan 武 芸 館 which means "House of the arts of wars", it can also be translated as House of martial arts. .

GABRIEL GARCÍA

THANKS

Most especially, the three authors of this study want to thank and congratulate the work of the teacher Juan Jose Lorenzo, for his great contribution and collaboration within the sphere of traditional Judo and Jujutsu. Thanks to his work we have been able to finish this work.

To the two instructors who perform the work of Tori and Uke:
Isabel Tomás Domínguez and Marisol García Muñoz, for giving the best of themselves for the benefit of tradition, the highest values of budo and for their great professionalism.

We would also like to thank all the teachers and budokas from whom we always receive love, support and collaboration.

Special Recognition & Thanks to:

Giuseppe Corbo, Martín Rubén Suárez, Ricardo Mercado, Jose Luis de Antonio, Jose María Lopez, Jorge Herrero, Dionisio de La torre, Francisco Jiménez, Massimiliano Vona, Cícero Melo, Nuno Santos, Sergio A. Vásques, Juan de la Fuente, Jose Balsalobre, Marisol García, Rafael León, Santiago Hernández, Jorge Rueda, Tomas Machín, Angel L.Lorenzo, Filip Rubinek, Miguel Fernandez, Takery, Jose Juan Gazquez, Fco Javier Donaire, Angel Soler, Ignacio Prado, Francisco Silvestre, Bill Cooley, Yumak Alonso, Belarmino Rodríguez, Francisco A. Marrero, Juan A. Saez, Ivan González, Francisco Herrera, Miguel A. Rodriguez.

TO ALL – OUR SINCERE THANKS

INDEX

INTRODUCTION

For many years now, we have established a firm commitment to spread the authentic legacy of Kodokan Judo founder, Jigoro Kano. Through conferences, interviews, seminars in several countries and several books published in 4 languages we have managed to reach thousands of people around the world who have known principles, katas and techniques that are forgotten or disused today. As we all know, Kodokan Judo has been redirected solely towards the sporting side, turning its back on many aspects that made Kodokan Judo a precious and complete art. A situation that the current international Judo leaders are not interested in reversing.

Our work of research, translation and verification has been hard, but thanks to our passion for the work of Jigoro Kano we have exposed much of what many teachers of Kodokan Judo and Jujutsu know and practice daily following the authentic legacy of Prof. Kano. This is not only limited to randori or shiai.

Some old studies and the unpublished work "Judo Kyohon" written by Prof. Kano in 1931 have been decisive and allowed us to develop many lines of research that we have materialized in several books published such as the aforementioned "Judo Kyohon", "Kodokan Judo Atemi Waza", "Tenjin Shinyo ryu Jujutsu", "Unpublished writings of the founder of Kodokan Judo", "The Lost Kata of the Kodokan Judo", "The Self-Defense of Kodokan Judo", "Goshin Jutsu Self-Defense" and "Traditional Kodokan Judo: The Method of Self-Defense of Kyuzo Mifune."

Thanks to these publications nowadays you can practice the Torite no Kata, Kime Shiki, Joshi Goshinho, Go no Kata, Mifune Soen Goshin Jutsu etc.

There are many Kodokan Judo teachers who received instruction directly from Jigoro Kano. Most became great teachers and ambassadors of art. Some of those sensei are recorded in history to have developed exemplary technique in both kata, randori and self-defense.

Those sensei were and still are a reference in the complete traditional Kodokan Judo.

In this study we addressed the method of self-defense for women created by the direction of Kodokan in 1943, which is why it was an official kata within Judo. Unfortunately, it has fallen into oblivion just as it has happened with other kata and groups of techniques. This method was developed by first level teachers, students of Jigoro Kano, some of them were later promoted to 10th Dan.

For this reason and for the technical richness of this method is why we encourage everyone to practice and promote it regularly in the dojos around the world.

Unfortunately, women continue to suffer all types of aggression regardless of the country where they reside, making necessary more than ever the in-depth study of specific techniques and skills so that women can repel an attack.

Undoubtedly, nothing better than to practice with seriousness and regularity the Joshi Goshin Ho to achieve this goal.

We wish you to enjoy this book and to know and practice the techniques of self-defense for women of Kodokan Judo.

THE AUTHORS

BRUCE R. BETHERS - JOSE A. CARACENA - GABRIEL GARCÍA

CHAPTER 1:
HISTORY AND TRADITION

The training in real combat and self-defense in all its forms have undoubtedly been the main objective of all the ancient Japanese schools of martial arts (Koryu Bujutsu).

With some exceptions, the study of bujutsu was intended primarily for men. Gradually the incorporation of women was gradually allowed during the 18th century, creating small groups of students that mainly came from a middle-high social class, or had family ties with high-ranking or prestigious samurai.

In general, women managed the houses and occupied their time in housework and in raising their children. His dedication to crafts and manual work was also frequent. However, sometimes they were recruited to fight in the different battles that took place in feudal Japan. Damyo claimed them and ordered his instruction in bujutsu. Depending on the clan where they belonged this situation could be something occasional that served the reasons of reinforcing the samurai garrisons or more commonly they could begin to be instructed when they were still girls.

JOSHI GOSHIN HO

In this case and from early ages, girls and adolescents also received training in martial arts. His specialty was the Yari (a spear with a straight blade) and the Naginata (spear with a curved blade).

Samurai women responded to the same standards of honor and loyalty as samurai men.

It is well known and documented the success of the onge bugeisha (female warrior) to infiltrate and perform tasks of espionage and obtaining information. In many ways the warriors used seduction to obtain their military objectives.

There are many examples of samurai women who fought with their husbands on the battlefield. The most famous was Tomoe Gozen, who fought against the Taira in the Gempei wars. In a famous battle he killed many men; the enemy leader tried to capture her and ripped a sleeve from her dress. Furious, she cut off his head and took it to her husband.

TOMOE GOZEN

Many writings and documents from a multitude of schools have come from the past, but it was not until 1914 that the first bujutsu book was published that was exclusively and exclusively dedicated to developing feminine self-defense, entitled "Fujin Goshin Jutsu"

This work was written by Nohata Showa and it shows some influence of Koryu Jujutsu and Kodokan Judo. Techniques of personal defense, location of vital points (Kyusho) and some techniques of projection and dislocation are present.

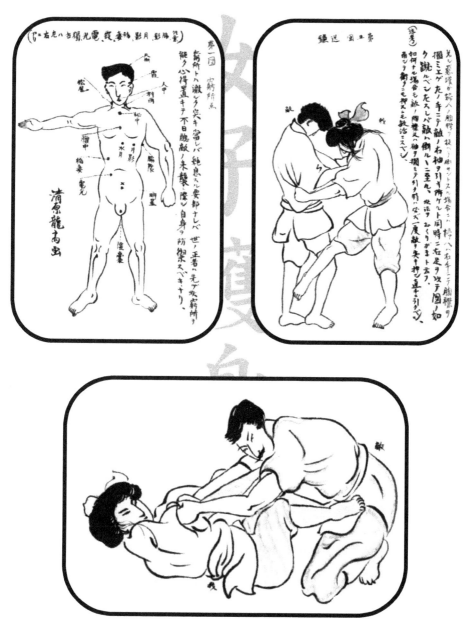

IMAGES OF THE FUJIN GOSHIN JUTSU BOOK OF 1914

SCHOOL OF BUJUTSU:
UNNECESSED IMAGES OF A PERSONAL DEFENSE
CLASS FOR WOMEN

With the end of the era Edo 1867 and the beginning of the Meiji Era, 1868 the Koryu JuJutsu or old schools of hand-to-hand combat, they began to accentuate their curriculum as far as personal defense was concerned. The term Goshin Jutsu began to be used more and the techniques of Shinken Shobu or real combat to life or death, were not lost of sight but everything was changing and with it the martial arts.

The great Master Jigoro Kano, was ahead of his time and as soon as he saw the opportunity to enter the woman in his Kodokan Judo, he did not miss the opportunity. Dedicating himself to the tutelage and teaching of young women who started in their Judo: the spiritual way or path of flexibility.

THE MASTER KANO IN GOSHIN JUTSU CLASS
THROUGH THE WORK OF THE KATA.

In the chronicles of his work promoting Judo Kodokan, it is narrated that his openness attitude, made him have many differences with Baron Pierre de Coubertain, when Kano Shihan promoted a great change in the face of the celebration of the Olympic Games.

In which, of course, wanted to give the right place to the woman as any other athlete.

KANO JIGORO SHIHAN, TEACHING IN THE JOSHI BU OR FEMALE
DEPARTMENT OF THE KODOKAN. ONE OF THE JUDOKAS IS
NORIKO YASUDA WITH HER PARTNER AYAKO AKUTAGAWA.

Jigoro Kano started giving classes to many women, in his own home
and he saw that they had great possibilities to understand his goals;
that new spirit that wanted to infuse Japanese Budo.
His first student, was Miss Sueko Ashiya and it was in 1893, when she
asked the teacher, to receive classes of her new JuJutsu method:
Kodokan Judo.

THE MASTER KANO IN FULL DEVELOPMENT OF A CLASS OF FOOT
JUDO, TACHI WAZA AND NE WAZA, JUDO SOIL IN THE KODOKAN
JOSHI BU.

Jigoro Kano, taught his wife and daughters and many acquaintances that experimentally, had the teacher investigate for the adaptation of his Judo so that women could practice it. The improvements in the health problems of many of them, the confidence and security that they were acquiring, led to the fact that in November 1926, the Kodokan Joshi Bu or Kodokan Women's Department, was opened for women to start in the practice of his new method.

JU NO RI, THE FUNDAMENTAL PRINCIPLE OF JUDO:FLEXIBILITY OVER BRUTE FORCE

To mention some of the women who contributed to Master Kano in the creation of this department and that women had a place in martial arts, include:

• Katsuko Yanagi, sister of Jigoro Kano, one of her first students and collaborators.

• Utako Shimoda, Japanese activist in defense of women's rights and pioneer in the adaptation of the educational system for the new times. He trained under the tutelage of Kano Shihan, for many years. They collaborated to take Kodokan Judo to schools for boys and girls.

UTAKO SHIMODA

TRAINING OF CHILDREN

• Noriko Yasuda, began his training in 1884. At 33 he suffered serious health problems so Master Kano gave him private lessons.

• Sueko Ashiya, began the practice of Judo in 1893; She was Kano's first student in his home.

• Ayako Akutagawa, was among the first three women enrolled in the Kodokan in 1926 and promoted to 1st Dan in 1934.

AYAKO AKUTAGAWA

• Masako Noritomi, started his training at the age of 10, was also among the first three Kodokan in 1926. He ascended directly to 2nd Dan in 1934, jumping the 1st Dan ladder given his qualities and became one of the First women to hold a high degree as an instructor in the Kodokan Joshi Bu.

• Katsuko Kosaki or Osaki, first woman 1st Dan, promoted to this degree in 1933.

• Masako Wada, another of the first women promoted to 1st Dan.

• Keiko Fukuda, granddaughter of Master Hachinosuke Fukuda first Master of Tenjin Shin'yo Ryu JuJutsu of Master Kano. She was invited to the Kodokan Institute in 1935 and spent her entire life dedicated to teaching.

• Hisako Miyagawa, Director of the "Oin Women's College", was promoted to 1st Dan in 1936 with 59 years of age.

Master Jigoro Kano in the center of the photo, celebrating an event of the Feminine Department or Joshi Bu of the Kodokan Institute, on September 30, 1937.In the photo he accompanies Master Kano and students, Instructor Handa Yoshimaru 8th Dan at that time.

The older daughter of Master Kano, Noriko Watanuki, was the coordinator of the new section of the Kodokan Institute, she only held an honorary degree of 1st Dan but she was full of enthusiasm to learn and coordinate the new martial movement that her father had seen good and in which I had high hopes.

THE MASTER KANO WITH HIS WIFE AND SOME OF HIS
CHILDREN.

A few years after the death of Jigoro Kano, the kata "Judo Goshin Ho"
was created. In current judo this kata is hardly practiced.

With the death of the great Master Kano in 1938, the Kodokan
remained without succession in the direction of such a prestigious
institution, for about ten months approximately.

It was in that same year when Jiro Nango, nephew of Kano Shihan,
assumed the presidency until 1946.

JIRO NANGO

Nango was a career soldier and went very far in his military powers, which earned him good status to have important influences within the Imperial Navy. Regrettably, his ultra-nationalist leanings were far removed from the way of thinking of his uncle, Jigoro Kano Shihan.

However, the new president saw that times were changing and that aspects such as self-defense techniques for Judokas should not be lost. So far, Katas of Self-Defense such as Kime Shiki and Kime no Kata were studied, complemented with the Seiryoku Zenyo Kokumin Taiiku no Kata, as physical education and practice of the Atemi Waza.

The Ju no Kata, was practiced, not only slowly, but also energetically, thus adopting a character of self-defense. That's why in 1943, he asked a group of teachers to create a Kata representative of the Goshin Jutsu techniques studied in the Kodokan Joshi Bu more in line with the new times that were lived, and that's where the journey begins in the elaboration of Joshi Goshin Ho.

The group of teachers composed between eight and ten kata specialists. the most known were:
-Kyuzo Mifune 10th Dan since 1937, technical manager of Joshi Bu.
-Noriko Watanuki, 1st Dan. Director of the Women's Department.
-Ariya Honda 8th Dan and Chief Instructor of Joshi Bu.
-Yoshinaru Handa 8th Dan.
-Fusataro Sakamoto 6th Dan.
-Hisako Miyagawa, 1st Dan.
-Keiko Fukuda 3rd Dan.

FUSATARO SAKAMOTO
SENSEI 8-DAN AND
SAKANO SENSEI AT EL
JOSHI BU

MASAKO NORITOMI 5TH
DAN, PRACTICING NE WAZA
OR WORKING ON THE
GROUND WITH MASTER
HANDA YOSHIMARU.

Among the judokas who assist in the realization of the technique, we can see a very young Keiko Fukuda. Keiko Fukuda was not an active part in the creation of the Kata but she did have a testimonial character in the whole process being a student and a great friend of Sensei Masako Noritomi.

Women suffered many aggressions and rapes were common, being an execrable fact, it had to be added that they contracted very serious diseases that for lack of the development of antibiotic measures, led to the loss of life of most of the victims of those abominable acts.

MASAKO NORITOMI

KEIKO FUKUDA

The objective of the Kodokan leadership was that the women were prepared to repel an aggression and enjoy a perfect state of health that was derived from the practice of Kodokan Judo.

PRACTICING ATEMI WAZA

STUDYING DIFFERENT TECHNIQUES OF GOSHIN
JUTSU THROUGH KATA

In these photos, we can see the practice of Shinken Shobu techniques or real combat in extreme situations of life or death, they continued practicing through the Kata.

But the techniques of Goshin Jutsu or self-defense, acquired a more updated character and were taught both within the Kodokan Institute and in schools.

YOUNG PEOPLE OF A FEMALE INSTITUTE, PRACTICING ATEMI WAZA.

YOUNG PEOPLE OF THE KODOKAN JOSHI BU, PRACTICING ATEMI WAZA.

Returning to the group of teachers, say that they were expert Judokas and that yes, not everyone had studied Koryu JuJutsu, they knew the details of the techniques of Goshin Jutsu or self-defense that formed an integral part of the training of Kodokan Judo at that time.

In fact, Mifune Sensei had created his own Kata of Goshin Jutsu techniques: the Mifune Soen Goshin Jutsu, practiced in his personal Dojo by all his students. The only master of the group that had a Menkyo Kaiden in Tenjin Shin'yo Ryu JuJutsu, was Fusataro Sakamoto and no doubt it had a remarkable influence on the development of the Kata.

On the other hand, Honda Ariya Sensei, came from a family with samurai roots but it is known, that he had not studied Koryu JuJutsu. Instead, he had training in Military Swimming or Suiei Jutsu. Probably, he had some contact with BuJutsu as far as hand-to-hand combat is concerned but it is not known for sure.

What we are certain that she already taught Joshi Goshin Jutsu or Female Self-Defense in the centers where she taught Kodokan Judo. But the research and training of the techniques of Goshin Jutsu, were commonplace in the old Kodokan Institute.

In the words of Master Keiko Fukuda, after the Second World War, the social climate was very dangerous and women easy prey for criminals of all kinds.

Three great Masters of the Kodokan: Kyuzo Mifune, Shuichi Nagaoka and Kaichiro Samura, the three 10th Dans, did not stop to investigate in the Goshin Ho methods and that also served so that the Kata Joshi Judo Goshin Ho, was created.

The young Masako Noritomi and Keiko Fukuda, attended as students to these research laboratories and watched as these great teachers meticulously tested all kinds of techniques.

Master Suichi Nagaoka had received instruction in the Takenouchi Saint Ryu JuJutsu line, a school of Koryu JuJutsu, derived from the Takenouchi Ryu; the oldest of all JuJutsu schools.

MIFUNE   NAGAOKA   SAMURA

We must not forget to mention that Master Haruko Nobuyoshi who, along with her classmates, also witnessed these studies and that she would become an important instructor in the Kodokan Joshi Bu.

The Nobuyoshi Sensei, demonstrating the Ushiro Dori technique belonging to the group Seigo Ho of the Kata Joshi Judo Goshin Ho. The Uke is Master Osawa 7th Dan back then.

Another Kodokan Master and direct student of Kyuzo Mifune, was Kazuo Ito, 8th Dan of Kodokan Judo.

Master Ito gave classes of Joshi Goshin Jutsu to the students that he had in the teaching centers where he taught and wrote a book that was translated into English.

KAZUO ITO

In fact, the book dedicated to the Female Self-Defense, was titled: Joshi Judo Goshin Jutsu and in this book are the Kata Joshi Judo Goshin Ho, Seiryoku Zenyo Kokumin Taiiku no Kata, Ju no Kata and a large chapter dedicated to Atemi Waza, Kyusho and Goshin Jutsu techniques in general.

The student who exercises Tori in the book, was Tsunako Miyake and in the role of Uke, Sato Shizuya who was Secretary of the International Department of the Kodokan Institute for his knowledge of the English language. He also systematized the Nihon JuJutsu self- defense method, guided by the Masters: Kyuzo Mifune, Kazuo Ito, Sumiyuki Kotani, Kenji Tomiki, Tadao Otaki, Kusuo Hosokawa and Takahiko Ishikawa.

Master Miyake became a great expert in Goshin Jutsu and Kodokan Judo at the hands of Master Kazuo Ito and companion of the young Professor at the time, Shizuya Sato.

TSUNAKO MIYAKE   SHIZUYA SATO

In the photo on the left, Tsunako Miyake with his Master Kazuo Ito, demonstrating a technique of Joshi Goshin Jutsu and on the right a movement of Ju no Kata.

Tsunako Miyake Sensei demonstrating Aikido techniques with Hideo Ohba Sensei.
Given the formation of Miyake Sensei, it is said that he was part of the personal escort of the Emperor of Japan.

In Europe, we cannot fail to highlight a great expert in Kodokan Judo, Tomiki Aikido and Goshin Jutsu; it is none other than the teacher Miwako Natsume. Established in France since the 70s and married to Mr. Le Bihan French Judo master, has represented a benchmark in making known the Joshi Goshin Ho between French Judokas and beyond the borders galas.

In a little book entitled: "Judo par Ceintures: le Judo féminin". The Sensei Natsume, shows some movements of the Seiryoku Zenyo Kokumin Taiiku and also of the Joshi Judo Goshin Ho, together with several examples of Atemi Waza apart from those included in the Kata.

MIWAKO NATSUME

The Joshi Judo Goshin Ho was completed in 1943, more than 70 years have passed, but certainly this specific method of self-defense is of great interest even today.

Studying it in depth acquires a formidable formation that enables you to repel many of the aggressions that unfortunately thousands of women suffer daily every day.

CHAPTER 2:
KATA JOSHI GOSHIN HO

The Joshi Goshin Ho is made up of a total of 18 techniques divided into 3 well differentiated groups:

1-TAI SABAKI HO: Methods of the displacements, practicing alone (Tandoku Renshu).
2-RIDATSU HO: Methods of escape or release, practiced with partner (Sotai Renshu).
3-SEIGO HO: Methods of escape and counterattack, practiced with partner (Sotai Renshu).

The in-depth study of this method reports a multitude of benefits, not only in the aspects of self-defense, but also in the acquisition of basic principles and foundations such as acquiring reflexes and agility, increasing coordination, learning to move properly and making turns and other movements with ease and efficiency.
In the years after the creation of Joshi Goshin Ho the instruction of this method was carried out in parts, that is, only the students who acquired sufficient skill in one group could move on to the next. This methodology ensured a correct learning and avoided unnecessary injuries.

USHIRO HIMO KUBI JIME (SEIGO HO) BY TSUNAKO MIYAKE

OBSERVATIONS AND ADVICE

OBSERVATIONS OF THE FIRST GROUP:
The way to move is more like a slide on the ground than at a normal pace, so you learn not to lift your feet too much when traveling. All the techniques of displacement will be carried out with the Kobushi closed fists (fist), except the number 5, which will be done with the open hand in Tegatana (sword hand).

All series of movements can be repeated twice on each side. In exercise 8 you will never forget the Kiai (scream) with the knee Atemi (Hiza Ate or Hizagashira Ate).

OBSERVATIONS OF THE SECOND GROUP:
Keep the Metsuke look in Uke (aggressor) at all times, as long as the aggression allows it. Keep the alert spirit at all times, Zanshin.

The serious attitude and energetic movements executed with force and speed are of great importance for release of the grips and the effectiveness of the defense. Although only liberation techniques are executed, the counterattack attitude must be maintained at any time.

OBSERVATIONS OF THE THIRD GROUP:
In this group not only are techniques to release a grip, now it is also intended to incapacitate the aggressor. The observations in this group are the same as the previous group, adding to each Atemi (hit), the Kiai (scream).

Rapid reaction and a rapid and coordinated response between defense and attack are crucial to achieve the goal. Another important aspect is the correct application of the atemi waza and the location of the vital points (Kyusho).

Alternatively, to attacks directed at tsuirgane (testicles) you can also attack the vital points Suigetsu (solar plexus) and Myojo (Hypogastrium). Alternatively, you can hit Sekito instead of Hiza Gashira.

ATE DOKORO (NATURAL ARMS) AND KYUSHO (VITAL POINTS) PRESENT AT JOSHI GOSHIN HO

KOBUSHI

TEGATANA

KOBUSHI: The bones of the base of the index and middle fingers.

TEGATANA: Side of the hand, area near the little finger.

SEKITO: Front part of the sole.

HIJI: Central point of the bone of the elbow.

SEKITO

HIZA GASHIRA

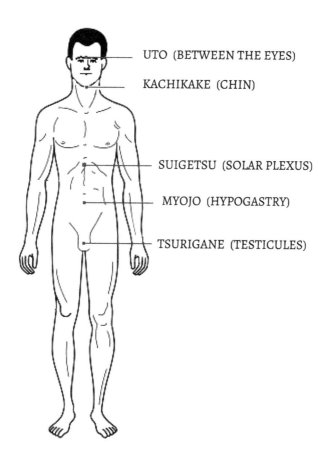

UTO (BETWEEN THE EYES)

KACHIKAKE (CHIN)

SUIGETSU (SOLAR PLEXUS)

MYOJO (HYPOGASTRY)

TSURIGANE (TESTICULES)

JOSHI GOSHIN HO

TAI SABAKI HO

1- TAI NO IDO. MIGI YORI, HIDARI YORI.
2- TSUGI ASHI. HOZEN, HAGO / MIGI YORI, HIDARI YORI
3- MIGI SABAKI, HIDARI SABAKI
4- MIGI MAE SABAKI / HIDARI MAE SABAKI
5- MIGI HARAI / HIDARI HARAI
6- MIGI MAWARI / HIDARI MAWARI
7- MAE SHIZUME / HIDARI SHIZUME / MIGI SHIZUME.
8- HIZA ATE. MIGI / HIDARI.

RIDATSU HO

9- KATATE TEKUBI DORI
10- RYOTE KATATE DORI
11- SHISHI GYAKU DORI
12- UDE KAKAE DORI
13- USHIRO DORI

SEIGO HO

14- UDE GYAKU DORI
15- USHIRO ERI DORI
16- USHIRO KUBI HIMO JIME.
17- USHIRO DORI.
18- KYOHAKU DORI

JOSHI GOSHIN HO

TAI SABAKI HO

1-TAI NO IDO MIGI YORI HIDARI YORI

OSHI GOSHIN HO

1-TAI NO IDO. MIGI YORI, HIDARI YORI.

Once the greeting is done, the left foot is advanced to open the Kata. Take a step with the right foot and the left foot advances to Shizenhontai to then move the left foot to Shizenhontai again. Slide the right foot to the right and slide the left one back to Shizenhontai, remaining in that position. Slide the left foot to the left and slide the right foot again, to Shizenhontai.

Repeat this series twice on each side.

JUSHI GOSHIN HO

TAI SABAKI HO

2-TSUGI ASHI HAZEN HAGO MIGI YORI HIDARI YORI

JOSHI GOSHIN HO

2-TSUGI ASHI. HOZEN, HAGO / MIGI YORI, HIDARI YORI

From Shizenhontai, we slid advancing the right foot followed by the left three times.

Then we slide backwards with the left foot, followed by the right foot, until we adopt the Shizenhontai posture.

The series of movements is repeated twice on each side.

TAI SABAKI HO

3-MIGI SABAKI HIDARI SABAKI

JOSHI GOSHIN HO

3-MIGI SABAKI, HIDARI SABAKI

From Shizenhontai, it is pivoted circularly with the right foot 90 degrees backwards leaving profile to return again to Shizenhontai. From Shizenhontai, it is pivoted circularly with the left foot 90 degrees back. Staying in profile to return again to Shizenhontai.

This series of movements is to be repeated twice on each side.

TAI SABAKI HO

4-MIGI MAE SABAKI HIDARI MAE SABAKI

JOSHI GOSHIN HO

4-MIGI MAE SABAKI / HIDARI MAE SABAKI

From Shizenhontai we take a circular 90-degree step with the right foot, followed by the left foot to move to profile and then return to Shizenhontai. From Shizenhontai we take a 90-degree circular step with the left foot, followed by the right to move to stay in profile and then return to Shizenhontai. Repeat this series twice on each side.

TAI SABAKI HO

5-MIGI HARAI HIDARI HARAI

JOSHI GOSHIN HO

5-MIGI HARAI / HIDARI HARAI

From Shizenhontai, advance the left foot and raise the right hand, Migi Katate Age, in Tegatana (sword hand). To move forward with the right foot and divert downward an attack on the lower body train. From Shizenhontai, advance the right foot and raise the left hand Hidari Katate Age in Tegatana (sword hand), To move forward with the left foot and deviate downwards an attack to the lower body train.
This series can be repeated twice for each side.

TAI SABAKI HO

6-MIGI MAWARI HIDARI MAWARI

JOSHI GOSHIN HO

6-MIGI MAWARE / HIDARI MAWARE

From Shizenhontai, swing 180 degrees to the right with your right foot until you are on your back and back in the opposite direction to the starting position. From Shizenhontai, swing 180 degrees to the left with your left foot until your back is turned and back in the opposite direction to the starting position. Repeat this series twice on each side.

TAI SABAKI HO

7-MAE SHIZUME HIDARI SHIZUME MIGI SHIZUME

JOSHI GOSHIN HO

7-MAE SHIZUME / HIDARI SHIZUME / MIGI SHIZUME

From Shizenhontai, the left leg is delayed and both arms extend to the height of the shoulder line. Next, Tori would bend forward and return to the starting position. Repeat movement from Shizenhontai but towards the left diagonal, returning to the starting position. Then repeat the movement from Shizenhontai but towards the right diagonal.

TAI SABAKI HO

8-HIZA ATE MIGI HIDARI

JOSHI GOSHIN HO

8-HIZA ATE. MIGI / HIDARI

From Shizenhontai, knees with the right leg, returning to the initial position and then with the left knee. To finish in Shizenhontai again. Repeat this series, twice on each side.

RIDATSU HO

9-KATATE TEKUBI DORI

JOSHI GOSHIN HO

9-KATATE TEKUBI DORI

After the greeting, Tori and Uke turn without turning their backs to the Shomen and they go to both sides to leave the objects they carry and then they are placed at 1 meter. Uke advances his left foot and grabs Tori's left wrist with his right hand. Tori lowers his center of gravity to follow the direction of the grip toward the thumb and forefinger of Uke's hand, freeing himself from the grip by advancing the left foot and bringing the left elbow towards Uke.

1

2

3

4

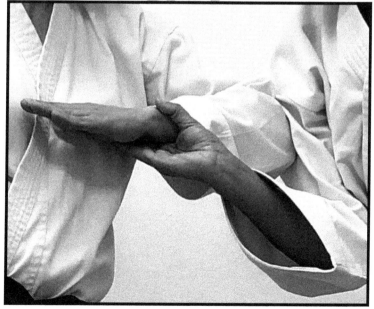

DETAIL

RIDATSU HO

10-RYOTE KATATE DORI

JOSHI GOSHIN HO

10-RYOTE KATATE DORI

Uke advances his right foot and goes to grab Tori's right wrist with both hands, Tori lowers his center of gravity, advances his right foot and stretches the fingers of his right hand well. Tori raises her hand, taking advantage of the turn of her hips in the same direction to overtake her left foot and move to the right side of Uke. Turning the hand so that the edge of the hand, begins to cut the grip of Uke. Releasing with a decisive cut the prey of the two hands of Uke.

1

2

3

JOSHI GOSHIN HO

4

5

RIDATSU HO

11-SHISHI GYAKU DORI

JOSHI GOSHIN HO

11-SHISHI GYAKU DORI

Uke advances with his right foot and grasps with his right hand, the fingers of Tori's left hand. Starting to raise the fingers, forcing them. When Tori feels the possible dislocation of his fingers, he takes a step back to the pair of a dry pull of the fingers that are being held. In this way, he manages to free himself from the grip.

1

2

3

4.

DETAIL

RIDATSU HO

12-UDE KAKAE DORI

JOSHI GOSHIN HO

12-UDE KAKAE DORI

Face to face, Uke moves to Tori's left, hugging Tori's left arm with her arms. Uke advances the left foot, pulling Tori forward the same foot, using his left foot as an axis, pivots 90 degrees to face Uke and pushing the left elbow of it, stretching his left arm. Tori begins to unbalance Uke. Tori continues to push Tori's left elbow, until it moves with a twist to his left.

1

2

3

JOSHI GOSHIN HO

4

DETAIL

RIDATSU HO

13-USHIRO DORI

JOSHI GOSHIN HO

13-USHIRO DORI

Standing face to face, Uke moves to stand behind Tori's back and holds Tori's body over her arms. Tori performs the Mae Shizume displacement technique to then lower her center of gravity and begin to pass under Uke's arms. Once released from the prey, Tori and Uke rotate so that they remain in profile.

1

2

3

4

5

SEIGO HO

14-UDE GYAKU DORI

JOSHI GOSHIN HO

14-UDE GYAKU DORI

Tori and Uke meet face to face and Uke goes to Tori's left side in order to grab Tori's arm and dislodge him. Once on the left side, Uke proceeds with the dislocation, Uke advances on the left foot and Tori the right, Uke advances his right foot and Tori the left. Taking advantage of that step, he pivots and throws a fist Atemi, Kobushi Tie to Uke's face.Tori controls Uke's right hand and nulls it down. Tori takes Uke's left forearm with both hands. Tori is placed laterally with respect to Uke, locking his left elbow and passes to his back to give an Atemi with the palm of the hand, Tenohira Ate Uke; without releasing the grip of the arm.To finish, Tori and Uke begin to walk, advancing first the left foot. After the right, to stay sideways and keep turning until Shizenhontai, as shown in the photos.

1

2

3

4

5

6

7

DETAIL

DETAIL

83

SEIGO HO

15-USHIRO ERI DORI

JOSHI GOSHIN HO

15-USHIRO ERI DORI

Uke grabs with his right hand, the collar of his jacket. To which Tori responds with a 180 degree turn to his right and applies an Atemi, ascending Kobushi Ate on the chin (Kachikake). Tori slaps Uke's arm and they move away from each other.

1

2

3

JOSHI GOSHIN HO

4

5

SEIGO HO

16-USHIRO KUBI HIMO JIME

JOSHI GOSHIN HO

16-USHIRO KUBI HIMO JIME

Uke prepares to strangle Tori behind with a rope. Tori responds by turning to her right and applying an Atemi, Kobushi Ate, ascending directed to the chin, blocks with both hands the elbows of Uke and applies an Atemi with the knee, Hiza Ate. Finishing the defense, pushing Uke to the level of his armpits, being able to free himself from the prey.

1

2

3

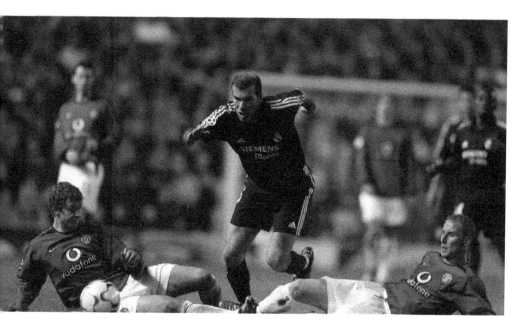

Lightning Source UK Ltd.
Milton Keynes UK
UKHW021010101019
351348UK00007B/185/P